THE BROCKHAMPTON LIBRARY

CW01651641

Teller

BROCKHAMPTON PRESS
LONDON

© 1996 Geddes & Grosset Ltd, David Dale House,
New Lanark ML11 9DJ.

This edition published 1996 by Brockhampton Press
a member of Hodder Headline PLC Group.

All rights reserved. No part of this publication may be reproduced, stored in a retrieval system, or transmitted, in any form or by any means, electronic, mechanical, photocopying, recording or otherwise without the prior permission of the copyright holder.

ISBN 1 86019 277 7

Printed and bound in the UK

Contents

Introduction

There are many secrets to be revealed through the ancient arts of fortune-telling.

The most popular and perhaps the most immediately recognisable is that of crystal gazing – a divination which has been practised from the earliest times.

The first chapter of this book looks at Clairvoyance and Crystal gazing, tracing its history through to modern times, and gives a background to the practise and its interpretations.

In the same way Tea-Leaf Fortunes introduces a favourite, lighter form of divination with an explanation of the procedure to be followed for reading the leaves, with discussion of the symbols and their meanings.

Dice and Dominoes have been used for many games of chance and fortune though history. Instructions are clearly laid down with common interpretations to allow this form of divination to be tested. Fortune-Telling by Numbers, Weather Fortunes, The Months and their Fortune complete this volume which will introduce you to ways of taking control of your life in ancient ways perhaps new to you.

Clairvoyance and Crystal Gazing

Among the many methods of divination, the most popular is that of crystal gazing, said to be convenient, consistently reliable and quick and is perhaps less distressing to the clairvoyant than many other methods.

This mode of divination has been practised from very early times with the aid of a crystal globe, a pool of water, a mirror, or indeed any transparent object. Divinations by means of water, ink, and such substances are also known by the name of hydromancy. Crystal gazing could be a very simple or a very elaborate performance, according to the period in history in which it was practised, but in every case the object is to induce in the clairvoyant a form of hypnosis, so that he or she may see visions in the crystal. The "crystal" most in favour among modern crystal gazers is a spherical or oval globe, about four inches in diameter, and preferably a genuine crystal; but as a crystal of this size and shape is necessarily expensive, a sphere of glass is frequently substituted, and with very good results. It must, however, be a perfect sphere or flawless oval, highly polished, and held in an ebony, ivory or boxwood stand.

Among the Hindus, a cup of treacle or a pool of ink served the same purpose.

Precious stones were very commonly used by crystallomancers in the past, the favourite stone being the beryl in pale sea green or reddish tints.

By the ancients, crystallomancy was practised with a view to the invocation of spirits, and very elaborate preparations and ceremonials were considered necessary. The early practitioners had to be of pure life and religious disposition. For the few days immediately preceding the inspection of the crystal, the fortune-teller washed frequently, and was subject to strict religious discipline, with prayer and fasting.

The crystal, as well as the stand on which it rested, had to be inscribed with sacred characters, as had the floor of the room where the invocation was to take place. Then, and now, a quiet place is suggested for the purpose, where the clairvoyant is free from all distraction and disturbance.

As well as these states of solitude and cleanliness, there is the question of the mental attitude to be considered, and this is no less important than the material preparations. A perfect faith was considered to be an essential condition of success. If the clairvoyant was to be accompanied by one or two of his friends or observers they also had to conform to the same rules and be guided by the same principles.

The time of the invocation was chosen according to the position of the heavens of the various planets, all preparations having been made during the increase of the moon. All the instruments and accessories used in the performance – the sword, rod and compasses, the fire and the perfume to be burned on it, as well as the crystal itself – were consecrated prior to the actual ceremony taking place.

During the process of invocation, the clairvoyant faced the east and summoned from the crystal the spirit desired. Magic circles previously were drawn on the floor, and it was desirable that the crystallomancer remain within these for some little time after the spirit has been dismissed. It was thought to be essential that no part of the ceremonial be omited, otherwise the event would be a failure.

Later, the view was developed that all such elaborate ceremonies were unnecessary, and that the *magnes microcosmi*, the magnetic principle in man, was in itself sufficient to achieve the desired object. In due course, though the ceremonial was not abolished, it became decidedly less imposing. If the person on whose behalf the divination was to be performed was not himself gifted with the clairvoyant faculty, he looked for a suitable medium, the best for the purpose being a young boy or girl, perfectly pure and innocent. Prayers and magical words were pronounced prior to the ceremony, and incense and perfumes were burned. Sometimes the child's forehead was anointed, and provided with suitable clothing for the impressive nature of the ceremony. Some writers mention a formula of prayers, known as *the Call*, which preceeded the inspection of the crystal. Finally, it was handled over the medium. The first indication of the clairvoyant vision was the appearance of a mist or cloud in the crystal. This gradually cleared away, and the vision made its appearance.

Modern crystal gazing is carried on in much the same manner, though the preparations are simpler. The crystal is spherical and of the size of an orange; when in use it may be held between the gazer's finger and thumb, or, if the end is slightly flattened, placed on the table; alternatively it may be held in the palm of the hand against a background of black cloth. The operation may be more easily carried out in subdued light. A medium or clairvoyant person acts as the seer and if the divination be made for anyone else it is advisable that he or she be allowed to hold the crystal for a few minutes before it is passed into the hands of the clairvoyant.

The object of crystal gazing is, as has been said, the induction of an hypnotic state giving rise to hallucinations, the reflection of light in the crystal forming focal points for such hallucinations. The value of elaborate ceremonials and impressive rituals lies in their potency to affect the mind and imagination of the seer. So far, the mystery of the crystal vision is no mystery at all. But the remarkable frequency with which, according to reliable witnesses, visions seen in the crystal have tallied with events happening elsewhere at the same moment, or even with future events, is a fact for which science has not yet found an adequate explanation.

It has been suggested that if telepathy operates with greater freedom during the hypnotic state, so it may be also with the self-induced hypnosis of crystal gazing. And this, though it cannot be said to cover the entire ground, is perhaps, on the whole, the best explanation on offer. There are many well-attested cases where the crystal has been successfully used for the purpose of tracing criminals, or recovering lost or stolen property. The telepathic theory, however, will hardly apply to these instances where events have been witnessed in the crystal before their actual occurrence. Such mysteries as these must be left to the art of the psychical researcher to unravel.

Clairvoyance, originally a French word, means the ability to see clearly. The reason so few people possess this extraordinary psychic faculty, is because many human beings seem incredibly blind, deaf, and insensitive to anything beyond the ordinary emotions.

The power of prophecy and acute intuition is a sixth sense which most of us have in a slight degree which often remains dormant and uncultivated.

Clairvoyance has often been mistaken for superstition or wilfully imposed and cunning deceptions, and it is difficult for many people to believe that it is founded on science and truth.

It has stood firm through the ages in spite of the quackery of wizards, the paraphernalia of sorcerers (used to inspire fear and awe in the uninitiated), the sneers of those of material minds. All of us at some time or other have felt the control of that still small voice, potent and penetrating as conscience, which comes, unaccompanied by earthquake or fire, to instil us with awe, joy, extreme sadness, or warning at some critical juncture of our lives; often anticipating, with power greater than speech can convey, some event that concerns our well-being.

Why this power should be deemed more extraordinary or mysterious than the senses of sight, hearing, smell, and touch which, even to those thoroughly familiar with the anatomy of the human body, remain steeped in mystery, it is difficult to say.

Science teaches that a million delicate sounds escape the ear and brain, and as many minute exquisitely fashioned atoms escape the eye.

A magnifying glass reveals the marvellous structure of insects and microbes invisible to the naked eye, and it is only by means of a telescope that the beauty of the stars is discerned; in this way the developed power of clairvoyance can be called the magnifying lens of the soul.

It is perhaps because this lens is dull and misty that we fail to see.

The history of ages and a great deal of our most cherished literature prove its existence.

Many of the stories and prophecies of the Bible are founded on clairvoyance. People were simpler and more trusting then; for this reason it is said that visions and clear sight were granted to them.

Pilate's disregard of the warning conveyed in his wife's dream, affected the whole course of Christianity, and the Bible abounds with examples of the disasters that befell those who disobeyed the spiritual promptings sent to them.

Colour and Character

Clairvoyance teaches that everybody has a distinctive colour, which conveys more of character and personality than any word or action. The shades of these colours vary according to temperament, and are as much concealed from untrained vision as the million tints composing the gold purple and green bands of the rainbow.

Optimistic people give out a pale blue aura.

Large minded progressive people, a pale green.

Pessimistic worried people, grey.

Ill-health in mind or body, dark green.

Kindly benevolent, humane people, pink.

The thinker and scholar, deep blue.

The degraded, brown.

The passionate and bad-tempered, red.

The ambitious, orange.

The lover of beauty in art, yellow.

These colours, however, although providing the key to the character, are subject to constant changes. Our moods sway and change our thoughts according to the happenings that affect us.

For example, bereavement or anxiety has power to transform the blue aura of the optimistic temperament to grey, and this temporary change of colour studied alone may puzzle the clairvoyant, and lead to a false diagnosis of character.

In order to prevent this, the seer should request some article constantly worn by the inquirer to be made available; the older and shabbier it is the better. A glove, an everyday tie or a ring constantly worn are equally valuable by which to discriminate between the temporary and habitual aura peculiar to temperament.

For example, when a man's glove emits a pale blue aura, in contradiction to the grey of his own personality, the deduction is that he is naturally of a hopeful and cheerful tendency, but that some mental anxiety or bereavement causes the grey, deep or pale, according to the depth of emotion dominating him.

The reason for this difference of colours is that the glove is, as it were, saturated with the essence of his normal disposition, while the colour of his character has been changed by circumstances or environment.

People of erratic temperament possess an aura of many and constantly changing colours, but those whose calm never varies maintain only one.

A few people are aware of the tones of their aura, and are therefore keenly sensitive to the influence of their surroundings.

They will be quite miserable if the paper on their walls, or the materials of their clothes, clashes in colour with that of their character; while they are at their best and happiest surrounded by the tints that blend or contrast harmoniously.

The clairvoyant will possess six key qualities:–

1. The power of magnetism.
2. Mental health and influence.
3. Physical health and cleanliness.
4. Moderation in food and drink.
5. The power of discerning the aura and interpreting its colours.
6. Freedom from all bad habits.

In advanced clairvoyance the use of the crystal for vision is designated by many seers as "clap-trap" thought to be a vulgar "playing to the gallery." It is known to be bad for the eyes to gaze at any shining article for too long a period, yet in clairvoyance there is no doubt that it aids the concentration of sight and thought.

By means of crystal gazing the seer creates and becomes subject to the influence of auto hypnosis—that is, the ability to become entranced which veils his or her own personality forming a link to the client.

The surface of the crystal gradually reflects images, and subconscious impressions conveyed by and vital to the individual whose past, present, and future are being revealed.

Sympathy and intuition merge the gazer's aura with the temperamental colouring of the client. The seer's magnetic force creates further powers, while the sixth sense is the nucleus about which these are bound.

No student of clairvoyance can be successful in discerning character and personal emanations of colour unless disciplined by simple rules which should govern his or her life.

Excessive eating, drinking, over-indulgence in any form, self-indulgence, bad habits, and drugs destroy this delicate sixth sense.

A lack of sincerity and integrity result in the rapid decline of its power.

The body and mind must be pure and of perfect

mental and physical balance.

In consulting a clairvoyant the client should be serious, earnest, and trustful that the truth will be heard. Frivolity, incredulity, or idle curiosity form a thick crust between the mind of exponent and inquirer, which prevents the penetrating of thoughts and vision, strain the powers, and result in disappointment.

The clairvoyant should be approached in the same way in which one visits a doctor or solicitor, and there must be no determined reserve to conceal thoughts and character in the mind.

Clairvoyance in a room full of people is extremely difficult—indeed impossible, unless the onlookers can keep perfectly quiet.

It is always better to be alone with the inquirer in a small room where traffic noises do not penetrate, provided only with the necessary furniture, kept clean and fresh, airy, and well lighted.

The crystal should never be touched by any one except the clairvoyant, and must be kept free from spots and smudges. A black silk handkerchief round its globe will be a help to divination by preventing the reflection of lights.

There may be, especially to beginners, temptations to pose as the possessor of supernatural powers—to make passes over the crystal, light wax tapers, burn perfumes, and murmur incantations—but these methods, although employed by the ancient prophets, are of no aid to the modern seer. Indeed, they do harm by appealing to the senses and superstitions, and, being a mere affectation, are unworthy of that sixth sense and harmful to it.

The simpler the manifestation, the more assured the clairvoyant may be of arriving at the truth.

Self-confidence, an absolute belief in the gift, and faith in method must rule.

The seer does not endeavour to avoid exertion of the nervous forces by discreetly "pumping" the inquirer as to ways and means, but takes a delight in silent investigation.

The clairvoyant should come to the task fresh and buoyant, bubbling with enthusiasm. At the slightest sense of tiredness the seer should halt all efforts, as it is extremely harmful to apply any force or strain to this abstract power.

Physical fatigue and excitement must be avoided, for these lead to jangled nerves, sleeplessness, and finally an inability to isolate the mind from the orbit of our own concerns to the sphere of others.

The processes that occur in crystal-gazing are thought transference and telepathy. A communication of ideas is set up between the prophet and client, and the mirror-like surface of the crystal is the medium by means of which innate thoughts are reflected.

As far as possible, the clairvoyant submerges his or her own personality in that of the inquirer, putting himself in his or her place. Profound silence brings about the sense of atmosphere and aura, and by these means, and an intent gazing into the crystal, visions originate.

The crystal is supposed to be the magic bridge which gulfs the chasm fixed between itself and the spiritual world. In the iron it contains are situated the collective and culminating forces.

Mists of white, green, blue, and violet tints are symbols of good fortune and happiness; black, yellow, and red are warnings of disaster.

When the mists disperse and gradually ascend to the surface, the clairvoyant may reply to any question in the affirmative; mists that descend to the bottom are negative signs.

Images that develop to the left of the clairvoyant are real; those on the right are purely symbolical.

It will be seen from the above that in order to apply oneself to the achievement of reading the secret depths of mind, character, talent, and circumstances, it is necessary to possess the ability to become separate from material surroundings and allow the spirit to dominate the body.

This can only be achieved by hypnotising oneself. Clairvoyance is based on certain forms of this semi-somnolent state, for, just as in hypnotism, the mind reigns supreme over matter and becomes isolated by means of an object, so, in clairvoyance, a waking trance is brought about by fixed gazing into the crystal.

However, there are other methods of inducing this state, some more and some less difficult in manipulation, until constant practice and experience have made them a habit.

For the reason that long gazing at a bright surface is harmful to eyesight, many clairvoyants prefer to create visions without the use of a crystal.

Words repeated over and over again have a mysterious power of isolating the sixth sense from the rest.

For example, the word AUM is extraordinarily symbolical. It stands for three influences:–

A = the Objective.

U = the Subjective.

M = the Eternal.

These are the kingdoms in the heart of man.

The Objective, being the natural surroundings of objects and events which we all can feel and see.

The Subjective, being the realm of influences the degree of which is felt according to the perception and training of our spiritual forces; too often vague and illusive, because most of us ignore its existence.

The Eternal World, being that state to which the subjective world, in its highest state of development, leads this word repeated, slowly and steadily at first, and then at great speed, to have a marvellous power to create as it were a vacuum between the spirit and body of the prophet.

The mind dwells on its meaning; the vibration of the different letters acts on the mind, and the gazer is carried by gentle stages to the very seat of his spiritual being.

It is when the seer attains this full development that large, clear, and deep perceptions of the client's character are granted, and it is possible to reveal facts concerning the client which in a normal state would be absolutely impossible

The sensation experienced is that of being plunged into space in which the senses of sight, hearing, and touch are transmuted to the brain and spirit.

The student will most probably be discouraged at

first at an inability to produce this state, but it should be remembered that hard work and perseverance are the attributes which all must give to attain perfection in any learning, art, or science.

One destined to become a great mathematician often stumbles in childhood with despair over the first addition sum, and the most distinguished musician has to do battle with the rudiments of music.

So it is in clairvoyance. Seemingly insuperable difficulties surround the novice who has never learnt to recognise the value and power of the sixth sense. Patience, a tranquil, determined mind, and not a little courage, are necessary in this branch of science. Time and growth work wonders in the persistent mind, and it will be seen that the obstacles gradually move aside, the curtain is lifted, and the strenuous seeker reaches that mature vision which he has formerly imagined dimly, if at all.

It is a good plan for the novice to ponder on his or her own name, and, shut away from all distractions, repeat it again and again aloud. The seer will gradually feel a sense of deepest mystery, for in that name is concentrated the riddle of existence. The blending of spiritual and material kingdoms lies behind it, and the material slips rapidly into obscurity.

Only when the heart is pure and worthy will the vision be granted —the clouds of bitterness, envy, hatred, and malice, which generally hide the precious jewel from the light, and render brilliance impossible, are discarded.

Everyone knows how difficult it is to control the mind, and keep it from mean and uncharitable thoughts. It is more rebellious even than the body, and influences it for good or evil.

Before all else, the clairvoyant must learn to discipline and constrain his or her thoughts.

A humble outlook, a longing for purity and singleness of purpose are needed to bring about the most noble qualities, and here it is that proper treatment of the body is invaluable.

Simple diet, early rising, daily exercise, constant isolation, and cultivation of good habits create the orbit for the higher faculties. These are the elementary rudiments of clairvoyance, and, unless they are mastered, the clairvoyant, no matter how diligent and persevering he or she may be in study and labour, will not succeed.

Tea-leaf Fortunes

The secret of success in this homely art consists of concentration, which enables the 'Seer,' who has an empty mind of all outside matters, to seize at a glance the symbols thrown up in the teacups and to read them intelligently, so that the Subject, or person whose cup is being read, can understand.

The cup must be passed direct to the Seer by the person whose cup it is; that is, he or she who has drunk the tea. If the cup passes from hand to hand before it reaches the Seer, the fortune will be confused and undefined, and most likely untrue.

It is also desirable that the Subject should sit near the Seer when the cup has been given up. But the cup ought to be turned over on to the saucer to allow for "tears" to be drained off the leaves before it is handed to the 'Seer.' It is extraordinary how tears, or drops of tea, *will* stay in the cup, however long it has remained turned over, on the saucer, *if* there is matter for grief in the fortune of the Subject.

Some Subjects turn the cup round three times and touch the edge of the saucer with the cup, "wishing the Wish of the Heart" as they do so. But unless there is a clear or outstanding Star near the top on the inner side of the teacup, one hears no more of this "Wish of the Heart." (Wishes properly belong to divination by Cards.)

The Seer or Reader picks up the turned-over cup from the Saucer, which the subject hands over.

You (if "you" are the Seer) hold the cup in your right hand. Note that the handle of the teacup is the House or Home of the Subject or "her place." For one whose interest is all in business, the handle may stand for "the Office"; for an actress it may mean "the Theatre," for a doctor, "the Surgery." But for the average man or woman you will do well to read it as "the Home."

The near or inner side of the cup, as you hold it in your right hand, is "the Fortune," the things that are happening or are sure to happen.

On the outer or farther side we read thoughts; things that may come, that are likely or possible, but that are now very much "in the air"; unfulfilled, uncertain. If you read the same person's cup to-morrow or in a week's time, there may be quite a different story to be read from the outer side of the cup.

Some seers read a month's time in the depths of the cup, dividing it into two, and reading the immediate fortnight that is coming from the top half, and the third and fourth weeks from now in the lower half of the cup's side. Happenings of a month ahead are near the bottom of the side. The very top is to-day. The rim is *now*. Close to the rim, by first post to-morrow morning! A leaf or sprig sticking out on the rim, startling news, *now*. Any sign sticking out implies surprise, even shock!

Note that the leaves or sprigs or tea-dust – any combination of symbols, in fact – that lie on the bottom of the cup stand for trouble, annoyance, anxiety, mishap, bad luck, misfortune. Even if it is a Star, it is a Wish or a "glory" that will cause the Subject more sorrow than joy. And drops, moisture, liquid, things that stand for "tears" – or if very wet, for "tears and sobs" – always cling to the bottom of the cup. Notice especially that whatever you read in the bottom of the cup is timed as NOW. This is all to the good. Your Subject's cup may be quite clear at the bottom tomorrow!

Sometimes, especially if the Seer is reading a person's cup for the first time, and more especially if they are meeting for the first time, the skilled reader will rule out all "time" and will read from the cup a fortune that goes far ahead and may cover the whole life of the Subject.

The most experienced reader of teacups cannot tell what it is that impels him or her to do this, but *does* know that he or she is actually and truly reading what is sure to come true, and *feels*, with the feeling that is stranger than all knowledge, that what is "seen" must be said. This rare and inexplicable state of mind looks beyond all symbolism. Symbols are no longer there; for the Seer is now really *clairvoyant*, seeing *nothing*, but "telling" of what is surely in the veiled future.

The Meaning of the Symbols

Sprigs are mostly people. Tightly curled sprigs are men, and more loosely furled ones, women. Upstanding, these are "straightforward" people; though if there is any kind of a weapon pointed at them, or from them, the message is "Beware." Sprigs set across are people who have been vexed.

Look at the near-by symbols to find out *why*. Sprigs set sideways are people who are not quite trustworthy.

People are also represented by **faces**, **initials**, and **signs**, which the subject must identify. Sprigs, and indeed all other signs explained here, are to be read as important or negligible, according to size and clearness. Signs that disappear almost as they are read, are true things that are ceasing to matter.

Dots are news, but of things of the mind, scholarship, science. Dots set as a triangle, a Wish, a successful but not exactly a material one. Dots are "fine" things, sometimes ideas.

Masses or **heaps** of tea-leaves are prosperity. The larger or higher they are, the more money or good luck is indicated. But masses in the bottom of the cup says that there is much anxiety even concerning what should be unmitigated good.

Stars are successes, desires fulfilled, "glory" achieved, startling success. In the bottom something in the nature of fatality accompanies the good happenings.

Rings, if small, mean business offers. If large, a proposal of marriage. Rings are always something that involves a question or offer. A circle with a letter near it says the offer will be conveyed in writing.

Part-Circles or **Half-Rings**. A ring formed of dots, not so definite an offer. A half- or a part-circle, not fully closed, an indefinite offer, or a half-question thrown out as a "feeler," or with some hesitation. The same rule as to smallness or largeness applies as to the complete ring; business if small, marriage if large.

Crosses. Things earned. A large, well-made cross tells of painful ambition realized. A small or ill-made cross implies obstacles, with danger of losses.

A cross beside a grave, a funeral. Near to a wreath of flowers, a death. Not "near," if there are no tears in the bottom of the cup.

Triangles. Prevention of ill. Trouble avoided. See symbols near, to read these more fully.

Squares also tell of safety from a feared danger. A deliverance. With a half-moon, danger of drowning escaped. But squares say that the Subject is, for the time being, "taking one step forward and two steps backwards." At best, is merely "marking time," even if the square is set in the clear of the cup's side.

Faces. Describe these to the Subject, say whether they appear to stand for men or women, old or young, sad or joyful people. The Subject must identify them. Sometimes the Subject's own face is formed clearly by dots; notice its position and the signs near it. But the fact that it is there, means that the day or the time is important.

Animals. Horses and dogs are friends. A lion, a powerful friend. A tiger, an unreliable rich man, not necessarily an enemy. Leopards, wolves, etc., are enemies. A cat or a cow, a deceitful woman. Monkeys are mischievous people, especially if they are grinning.

Birds, if they are in flight, say that news is

coming. A bird standing, not so good. A bird standing on one leg, plans frustrated, or things changed for the worse, since news was received.

Gardens. Flirtations.

A Baby. One expected. A cradle near it, all will be well.

Lines stand for distance. Two lines are journeys by train or car. A ship is a voyage. Cars, engines and such things stand for themselves; but notice how they are placed, and *where*.

Letters mean exactly what they are, also. A dot in the middle of a square or "long square" letter, tells of money by post. Dots set inside of small circles are also money through business or affairs.

Two hearts tell of an engagement; with a ring around them or near them a happy marriage. A CROWN over the joined hearts is a very auspicious sign.

Alphabet Letters are often thrown up in the teacup with astonishing clarity. These do not always stand for the initials of a name; they may indicate a town. But two or three capital letters together are, as a rule, initials of some one with whom the Subject ought to get into communication. Figures must be read in conjunction with the symbols near.

Enough has been said to show how the teacups

ought to be read. "The way to do it, is TO DO IT." A last word to the would-be Seer: Never hesitate to say what you see clearly in the cup you are reading.

If you are sincere (selfless) in the matter and the Subject is intelligent and anxious to know things, what you say is sure to be true or to come true. You may bank on this!

Dice and Good Luck

Dice have been used for many games of chance and fortune through history. In ancient Egypt and Classical Greece to the Far East, numbered cubes made of wood, glass, ivory or metal with their sides inscribed from 1 – 6 were popular for games and as a means of consultation. It was found through their medium that future happenings and events could be predicted.

Test this ancient form of divination:

Draw a chalk ring on the table or tablecloth. Three new dice and a new cup or shaker box are needed. All three dice must be shaken in the box, with the box held in the left hand.

If you throw all the dice outside of this ring, seek to know no more, and, above all, steer clear of quarells! One or two of the dice falling outside the ring indicates the same warning in a milder form. But the thrower, in this case, *may* throw again.

The following are the common interpretations of the sum total of the numbers on the faces which fall uppermost.

One – (that is one dice with one point and two with blanks) says: "Nothing doing!"

Two – Slight trouble, and rather a lack of good

news. Nothing to worry about.

Three – Good. Seize the chance that comes *today*. Your wish will be fulfilled, or a pleasing or happy event will take place.

Four – A disappointment; but it will turn out to be for the best.

Five – News of a death, but no surprise about the news.

Six – A marriage, news of which will surprise if not distress the thrower. Also a sign of the loss of a portion of wealth.

Seven – An omen of good luck. All will go well in the matter about which you are now anxious.

Eight – Disagreeable news through the post. "Sit tight." Better news will follow.

Nine – This is a good throw. Good happenings, but with some touch of scandal. Success in love, reconciliation of a quarrel or disagreement.

Ten – Uncertainty. Nothing worse. "Wait till the clouds roll by."

Eleven – Danger of loss of money through treachery. Also indicates illness of someone close.

Twelve – Some one seeks to involve you in an intrigue. Refuse to grant favours asked of you. There is danger of you being made a cat's paw. Do not act without seeking advice from a friend.

Thirteen – Warns you that an enemy seeks your downfall. Throw again, and if the number is higher, he shall not succeed.

Fourteen – Long voyaging, but not yet. Your travels shall prove profitable, but not easily profitable. Hope always. Also an indication of a new friendship to come.

Fifteen – Some domestic trouble. Examine whether there are people making mischief in your home. Sort it out!

Sixteen – You are going to be lucky in a matter of which you are not hopeful. Tell no one of your gains for a week after *you* know of them. Sixteen also warns you not to think too much about money. Other important things are being neglected by you. You shall not want money ever, but it will not supply the need of friendship.

Seventeen – Something very good indeed, unearned, unsought, even undeserved. You may well be thankful when this comes. Perhaps a suggestion or proposal from a stranger.

Eighteen – This is the very best throw of all. It tells of a high destiny. But beware of inconstancy when your luck is at its highest. "The full cup needs a steady Hand." Great luck and happiness.

Fortune Telling by Dominoes

A fairly unique accomplishment is to reveal the future using dominoes, and there is something sufficiently fascinating and mysterious about this method of fortune-telling to fill the uninitiated with awe at the powers of the exponent.

Each small oblong has its secret meaning by which some happening vital to the subject is illustrated. It is a simple matter to commit these to memory; and in this, as in other methods of divination, the fundamental principle is that of comparison and calculation.

The dominoes used range from double-six to double-blank, and by these are symbolised the various conditions of fate likely to befall mankind. The exponent places the dominoes on the table, and, having turned them face down proceeds to shuffle them. When this is done, the subject is requested to draw three pieces, one at a time. Between the choice of each, the dominoes should be shuffled.

The first supplies an impression; should it be drawn a second time, the impression becomes a conviction. The third, however, may lessen or wholly contradict its degree of importance, and this is where calculation and comparison in blending the signs are essential to a successful justification and interpretation of these symbols.

Do not draw more than three pieces at a single consultation, or indeed on the same day or you may well find that interpretations are misleading.

Double-six is an emblem of matrimonial happiness and financial prosperity.

Six-five is almost equally fortunate. Perseverance and concentration are rewarded by ultimate success.

Six-four implies a comfortable income, and secures happiness in marriage.

Six-three demonstrates that fate smiles upon love and marriage of the subject.

Six-two Prudence, hard work, and a certain amount of good luck, or exposure and shame for any wrong-doing.

Six-one promises two marriages to the young subject, the first of which will not be as happy as the second. Should the subject be of middle-age, this domino foretells the speedy arrival of good things and the fact that he or she will never be lonely and uncared for.

Six-blank is, unfortunately, a sign of great trouble – sickness, death, or heavy money losses.

Double-five tells that all achievements will be

rewarded with a large amount of success, but inordinate wealth is not prophesied.

Five-four is almost as unfortunate a draw as six-blank. Should a young girl lift it, it means that her future husband will be poor and leave her a widow. Further, he may be of extravagant disposition, in spite of his poverty.

Five-three indicates a tranquil and contented existence. Sufficient money and matrimonial affection of moderate strength, the couple being incapable of passionate devotion.

Five-two conveys a warning that love and marriage are destined to an unhappy termination.

Five-one tells of social popularity, but financial worries and losses.

Five-blank is supposed to demonstrate egotistical and avaricious characteristics, tendencies to swindling and intrigues, also a warning to remain unmarried.

Double-four The person who earns a livelihood by manual labour may regard this domino as a sign of future security and prosperity, but to those whose profession needs mental achievement it is rather disastrous. Troubles and disappointments await.

Four-three Matrimony and moderate income.

Four-two proclaims an early marriage and moderate income.

Four-one Wealth or many friends.

Four-blank A sure warning that single life will be the best and happiest. It counsels that any secrets imparted to another will be indiscreetly revealed.

Double-three Enormous riches.

Three-two foretells prosperity in matrimony, travels, and speculations.

Three-one Some danger and unhappiness. The necessity for acting with extreme caution in all matters.

Three-blank Domestic unhappiness-such as a quarrel or incompatibility of temperament of husband and wife. The absence of harmony in the home.

Double-two promises average happiness and income.

Two-one Two marriages, if the individual be a woman; financial failures to a commercial man.

Two-blank The intrigues of unscrupulous people will meet with temporary success. It also denotes poverty, and an indolent husband. The individual will return safely from all journeys undertaken.

Double-one An existence free from money

worries; peace and constancy in love and marriage.

Double-blank seems to favour the deeds of unprincipled people, and foretells want of integrity in lover and husband.

Fortune Telling by Numbers

We all have "lucky numbers" – but what are they and where did they come from? Numbers have a major part to play in our lives. They are everywhere! There are quite simple ways of identifying the special number that brings you luck on a certain day.

That a certain amount of character and fortune may be revealed by means of figures is a fact that can be tested for itself. The results achieved by this method of divination are truly astonishing, and can be very rewarding to the mathematician in the attempt to solve the riddle of human nature.

Certain groups of figures stand for different qualities. Those given in the table following are only a small portion of the whole, but they are sufficient for the beginner. Each letter of the alphabet has its accompanying digit, and each digit has its abstract condition:-

A	1	Passion, ambition, design
B	2	Destruction, death
C	3	Religion, destiny, the soul
D	4	Solidity, sagacity, power
E	5	The stars, happiness, graces, marriage
F	6	Perfect labour
G	7	Course of life, repose, liberty, success
H	8	Justice, preservation
I	9	Imperfection, grief, pain, expectation
J	600	Perfection
K	10	Success, reason, future happiness
L	20	Austerity, sadness
M	30	Fame, a wedding
N	40	Fetes, a wedding
O	50	Pardon, liberty
P	60	Widowhood
Q	70	Science, the graces
R	80	A cure
S	90	Blindness, error, affliction
T	100	Divine favour
U	200	Irresolution
V	700	Strength
W	1400	Perfection of Strength
X	300	Safety, belief, philosophy
Y	400	Long and wearisome journey
Z	500	Holiness
	800	Empire
	900	War, combats, struggles

The first thing to ask is the name of the subject. He writes it on a slip of paper, and next to each letter its accompanying figure. Here is the name, Dick James Smith:-

D	4	J	600	S	90
I	9	A	1	M	30
C	3	M	30	I	9
K	10	E	5	T	100
		S	90	H	8

Now they are added separately:-

Dick = 26 James = 726 Smith = 237

Add the three totals together:-

Dick	26
James	726
Smith	237
	989

The interpretation:-

900	War, combats, struggles
80	A cure
9	Imperfection, grief, pain, expectation.

The deduction being that Dick James Smith is endowed with a quarrelsome, headstrong nature, optimism, and inefficient will-power, which are destined to cause him trouble, loss, and misery.

Should the total of the names reach beyond 1390, the first digit must be subtracted, for example as in the name, Johannah Christine Whiting:-

Johannah		Christine		Whiting	
J	600	C	3	W	1400
O	50	H	8	H	8
H	8	R	80	I	9
A	1	I	9	T	100
N	40	S	90	I	9
N	40	T	100	N	40
A	1	I	9	G	7
H	8	N	40		
		E	5		
	748		344		1573

Total = 2665, take away the first figure, leaves 665.

600 Perfection

60 Widowhood.

5 The stars, happiness, graces, marriage.

The analysis showing that Johannah Christine Whiting's life will be a mixture of joy and sorrow, the latter borne by a courageous and tranquil spirit. Her integrity and attractiveness of character will, no doubt, bring her much love and friends.

If the fortune-teller has a good memory, the table

of qualities can be memorised, and a great aid to this is to practise with it perhaps analysing an author, statesman, or friend.

The fortune-teller's own name should reveal the fundamental truths of this method, and the analysis of people from history will show the distinguishing traits that have made them famous. For example, take Florence Nightingale:-

F	6	N	40
L	20	I	9
O	50	G	7
R	80	H	8
E	5	T	100
N	40	I	9
C	3	N	40
E	5	G	7
		A	1
		L	20
		E	5
	209		246

Total = 455

400	Long and wearisome voyage
50	Pardon and liberty
5	The stars, happiness, graces

The Numbers of the Alphabet

1	2	3	4	5	6	7	8	9
A	B	C	D	E	F	G	H	I
J	K	L	M	N	O	P	Q	R
S	T	U	V	W	X	Y	Z	

Now suppose your name is GLADYS TEMPLETON, write it downwards, like this:

G —	7	T —	2
L —	3	E —	5
A —	1	M —	4
D —	4	P —	7
Y —	7	L —	3
S —	1	E —	5
		T —	2
		O —	6
		N —	5
		Total =	62

You have added to each letter the number that stands for it. Their total value added together is 62. These two numbers add up to 8. You may bank on the importance of this 8, though there are some numerologists who would add to it certain mystic numbers which represent the day on which you make the calculation. The above is simple and it works out, strange to say, with striking results!

Finding your Lucky Number

Suppose you were born on the 16th June 1971:

Take the date of the month = 16.

Add the figures together	1 + 6 = 7
June is the sixth month, so add	6
Add the year of your birth	1971
	1984

Add these figures together (1 + 9 + 8 +4) = 22; and 22 (*ie.* 2 and 2) = 4

You will find that the figure 4 will turn out well for you; also any figures or any number in which it appears; or any of its multiples 8, 12, 16, as well as 49, 48, 94, 84; and especially 40, for the 0 intensifies any figure which it comes after.

Note that number 4 itself is not a very good number, although it will be favourable for you. People whose number is 4 suffer from "temper"—their own, as well as that of other people! To live in a house that is Number 4, to get a bus or train or theatre ticket in which 4 appears, more especially if the whole adds up to 4 or to a multiple of 4—this means happy travelling, auspicious enterprises. Wednesday being the fourth day of the week, will be lucky; April, the fourth month in the year also, especially if these be the day or the month of your birth.

But should you particularly dislike this number 4, it is up to you to change it. Some people add the day of the week's number to those given, Sunday being number 1, Monday number 2, and so on. This plan, if you adopt it, gives you a different number. You may work them both together, using one for business and the other for personal luck. But do not change entirely from 4, if this number is serving you well.

Weather Fortunes

We often have a need or desire to know what weather can be anticipated – perhaps when planning a holiday or a wedding, or there may be an important sporting event where the weather will play a part. There are many signs to note.

Insects, Birds, and Animals as Weather Prophets

Bats numerous at night, flying about longer than usual, indicate *fine, warm weather* on the next day. Fewer bats than usual in the evening, or when bats seek to enter sheds and houses, *bad weather tomorrow.*

owls crying, indicates *fine weather.*

ravens croaking in the morning, also *fine weather.*

ducks and **geese** rushing here and there and diving into the water when the weather is fine, *a storm is coming.*

bees making short journeys from their hives, promise *rain*. The same when they come back in swarms before night and without being heavily laden.

pigeons returning late to the pigeon-house, *rain on the following day.*

sparrows chittering freely and flocking together, *bad weather* is near.

hens rolling freely in the dust and **cocks** crowing in the night, *rain* is coming.

swallows skimming the surface of the water or flying close to the ground, tell of *bad weather*. But when they hawk very high, *continued fine weather*.

flies very restless and troublesome, *a storm is coming*.

gnats assembling before sunset into a circling mass, *fine weather*.

frogs croaking more than usual; **toads** coming out of their holes in great number; **worms** appearing on the surface of the soil; **moles** throwing up more earth than usual; and **oxen** and **turkeys** collecting together—all these signs foretell *heavy rain*.

cattle in the fields and **sheep** grazing particularly intently, say that *rain* is near. **Cattle** gathering together or remaining still grouped closely together tell that *thunder* is approaching.

cats licking their paws often and rubbing them over their faces, say that *rain* is near. The **cat** turning her back to the fire, tells of a *storm*.

cats with their tails up and seemingly electrified, tell of *windy weather* coming. **Pigs** restless and grunting loudly also promise *wind*; for pigs are said to be able to see the wind!

Weather and Inanimate Things

Rain may be expected when distant objects are seen more distinctly, or when they appear nearer than usual.

Wind may be expected if the coals in the grate of an open fire flare higher than usual, or flame actively.

Fair Weather when the flames burn evenly and steadily.

Frost when the flame is low and blue.

Wind, or some change in the weather, when bells are heard from afar.

Fine Weather when the smoke goes straight up.

Rain when it blows sideways as soon as it leaves the chimney.

Rain when smells, pleasant or offensive, are stronger than usual.

Violent Storms when the wind changes quickly and often.

Rain or a *Thaw* when salt, marble, iron, and glass become moist; when the wood of doors and windows distends and smells; and when corns on the feet become painful.

Weather and the Moon

"A Saturday's moon
Comes it once in seven years – comes too soon."

A new moon on Sunday is still more unfortunate; while if it comes in and goes out on a Sunday, we may expect the worst in the way of weather.

"If you point at the moon, rain will surely come!"

If the moon lies on its back in its first quarter, it is holding all the rain there is in its lazy curve, and will tip the whole lot out on earth when it straightens itself up. The moon seems to tell of nothing else but rain. If it has a lead-coloured ring, rain is promised. If the circle is red, wind with rain. If its halo is small, rain; if large, rain. But if there is no halo at all, then we can hope for fine weather.

Christmas Weather

"A warm Christmas, a cold Easter,
A green Christmas, a white Easter.
Christmas in snow, Easter in wind.
A light Christmas, a heavy sheaf."

If there is wind on Christmas Day, there will be much fruit.

"So far as the sun shines on Christmas Day, so far will snow blow in May."

If the sun shines through the apple tree on Christmas Day, there will be a good crop the following year.

Snow at Christmas brings a good hay crop for the farmer next year.

Strange Weather Coincidences

These appear to have been amply verified. 8th to 10th February are always cold days, however mild the weather has been up to the 8th. 11th to 14th April, 9th to 14th May, and 31st June to 4th July are also consistently cold. 12th to 15th July, which is St. Swithin's Day, are generally exceptionally hot. 1st to 8th August is a wet spell in nine years out of ten. 6th to 12th August is cold, followed by great heat.

The last few days of September are generally fine; and about 18th October we have, as a rule, a sweetly mild period known as "St. Luke's Summer." 6th to the 10th November is, as a rule, very cold; and December has a mild spell between the 3rd and the 8th.

The Months and their Fortune

January. Those who have a birthday in January are ambitious, proud, loyal, careless as to appearances; reserved, averse from showing their feelings. They have good business ability, if born in the second half of the month. The men are interested in engineering.

3rd and 13th January are among the twenty-eight outstanding good days of the year; these dates are auspicious for every one, though nobody ought to become engaged in this month.

The January-born people should dress in browns, greys, and black. They ought always to wear a garnet, which is the stone for their month. But it must be *given to them with love*, and not bought. They marry most happily partners born either in February or in July.

February. February-born people have good memories and are imitative and quick-witted; with acute understandings, although they are too apt to run away from "stiff thinking." They love dress and crave authority. They often suffer from rheumatic ailments.

They should wear purples, bluish purples and black if born in the first part of the month; those born in late February will find the red purples more lucky for them than the blues; and should always wear an amethyst. Those born in the first part will find 3 their lucky number; but those born the latter half may place their dependence on Number 9.

Tuesdays and Saturdays are good for the February-born, and March is a good month for them to embark upon new enterprises. They live happily with partners born either in January or in October.

March. These people are generous, impressionable, easy-going in money matters, apt to let good chances slip past them. But they *can* fight when they are really up against it, though they do not always, even then, hold what they gain. To wear the noble bloodstone, which is the month-stone of March, ought to help the March-born to cultivate that *steady* courage which they lack.

They may wear all-greens and will look well and feel happy when dressed in green and red together. Good days for the March-born are the 3rd, 22nd, and the 30th; the Fridays in their own month are propitious for them to embark on voyages or enterprises. March people are rarely very strong, though they are healthy.

March engagements do not last, as a rule. And the March people find happiness with those born either in September or in July.

April. The April-born are headstrong, erratic, fond of being in the limelight, fickle. Over-easily "up" and too soon "down" as regards their spirits. But they make good travellers, for they love change, and despise the common place and the ordinary in every connection.

They do not think things out, but they can, and do, advise others wisely. All too often they complicate their own lives and are unfortunate in their relationships with people in general, in spite of being very sympathetic.

They ought to dress in blues, greys, greens, and reds; but for evening wear, even when advanced in years, white is their most lucky wear. They should make important changes in April, and wear their own stone always, this being the glorious diamond.

They should marry someone they have known for years (hasty marriages are never good for the April-born), and should choose their life-partners from those born either in July or August or September.

May. May-born people are vivid, hopeful, and eager for adventure. They are somewhat obstinate, yet neither persevering nor patient; affectionate, but not generous. Destiny plays a big part in their lives;

it is the unexpected that happens to them. They are fascinating, with a flair for dress and a real talent for art in any of its manifestations. They do not easily learn by experience, yet they do not worry.

They ought to dress in vivid emerald green as much as possible, and wear their own emerald always. Good days are 4th and 20th May; these are for all. Good days for the May-born are the 4th, 22nd and 28th. The 9th of June is very auspicious for May people; and they should marry with partners born in May or in June, though the May-born join confidently and successfully with partners born in any month in the year.

June. Those who have birthdays in this lovely month are "born Rovers"; travellers, adventurers and pioneers, loving to wander far from the land of their birth. They are restless, magnetic, impetuous, over-apt to act on impulse; eloquent, dramatic, nervous, and, if born before the 20th of the month, inclined to be dreamers and even "work-shy." They influence other people but are not easily influenced themselves.

June is a favourable marriage month for any one. These dates are good for all: the 5th, 13th, 17th, 26th, 28th and 29th. The 3rd and the 8th are especially good for June-born people to start new ventures.

These born in June ought to dress in soft shades of red, yellow, and especially in white, and to wear an agate on the third finger of their left hands; for this is said to give them the power to attract to themselves the love of any one on whom they set their hearts. They marry most happily with persons born either in November or in December.

July. July-born people are generous and big-hearted, but they are over-anxious for pleasure and crave wealth, power, and authority. They are patient, persevering, and very thorough in all they do; not helpful in emergencies, for they require time in which to think things out. They never neglect appearances.

July-born people often have a hard time in their youth. They are great workers, also lovers of music of every description. They ought to take care of their lungs and check their love for flattery. They may dress in all the colours of the roses (never in blue, for who ever saw a blue rose ?), and wear a ruby all the time. Mondays and Thursdays through the year are favourable days for them, especially for love.

Good dates in this month are the 5th, 6th, 15th; the 15th and 18th July are particularly good for the July-born. They are happy with partners born either in January or in March.

August. August-born people are steadfast and truthful, but vindictive when rally vexed. Their strong sense of family leads them to shoulder burdens that do not properly belong to them, and they are all too often imposed on by the selfish and the lazy. This fact makes them become over-suspicious in later life.

They ought to dress in greys, drabs, and all the shades of tomato red, also deep yellows. They must take special care of their eyes; and wear a sordonyx, which is their own stone. An August woman rarely marries her first love, nor does an August-born man either. They are old for their years, and are most successful with partners older than themselves, preferably those born in May or in December.

18th August is a good day for everybody. The first Monday in this month is a day of evil omen.

September. Those born in September are full of nervous force, talented, but not really practical, with a special gift for languages; serious, sympathetic, and warmly affectionate, but not especially devoted, for their weakness is laziness, and they are over-disposed to be easily "sorry for themselves." As middle age approaches they may be tempted to intemperance.

July is lucky for them, especially for travelling. The numbers 5 and 6 will serve them well; 4th, 7th, 9th, 17th, 28th, and 30th September, are good days for all. Those born in the first week in September ought to wear primrose; in the second week, violet; in the third and fourth weeks, pale greens. But September people are generally happy when wearing blues, violets, and primrose yellow.

Their stone is the sapphire. They should choose a partner born either in March or in January.

October. The October-born are equable, sensible, fond of knowledge, but always practical and willing to use what they know, to their own advantage. Those born in the first half lack ambition, those born after 22nd October are more ambitious and capable of more patient work.

They are unwise in money matters. They dislike manual work, are averse to travelling, and they like to "go easy." They are constant in love and friendship, but over-apt to dominate those they love. October people are successful when working on the land, and will do well to acquire land of their own as they grow older.

The opal is the stone for October people. Unlucky for others it is lucky for them, and its wearer may always count on keeping the love of those whose love they have won so long as they wear this beautiful stone with confidence in its power.

January is a good month for the October people. 4th and 15th October are good days for everybody. Number 6 is lucky for the October-born, though number 5 is still more so for those born in the earlier half of the month. The October people always look well when dressed in greys and dark blues, for these are the colours of their stone; but reds and red mauves and pinky reds will also induce a woman to feel happy, especially in the evening. Their life partners should preferably be born in February or March, or July or August.

November. The November-born are reckless, extravagant, discontented; riotously happy or miserably depressed, fond of adventure, fond of spending as well as fond of giving, fond of luxury, of the good things of the table, and of "high-life" generally. They are clever and far-seeing in worldly affairs, and are only unwise when they love.

They ought not to marry too early nor too "easily." The November people are "great givers" both in love and friendship. When happily married, which is rare for the November-born, they make devoted wives and husbands, but are over-strict parents.

They should dress in yellow, with shades of golden brown, for these are the colours of their birthday stone, the glorious topaz. They ought to live on plain food and "stick to hard work and cold water." June is the best month for November people, and Friday is their best day. Lucky days for them in love matters are Wednesdays and Saturdays. Good days in November, especially for those born in this month, are the 6th, 9th, 15th, and 23rd.

Since marriage either makes or mars the passionate November born, their partners ought not to be much older nor yet far younger than they are; and they should, if possible, be persons born in October or in June.

December. Those born in December put business before love, especially as they get older. They do not easily forgive any wound to their self-esteem, and should resolve to think generously as well as to act generously. They are not very strong and, as they look well, they do not get much sympathy in illness. December people do not easily recover from ill-health.

The December women are too apt to get into a rut and to stay there. They love to help, to give, and to advise others. October is always a lucky month for the December-born people, and Tuesday is their best day. They should marry either on a Tuesday or a Friday. New enterprises entered into on either the 5th, 6th, 9th, 17th, 23rd, 25th, or 28th will turn out well.

31st December is the only "bad day" in this month. December people ought to dress in light blues and pinks; to see that they do not overtax their strength; and always to wear a torquoise, which will turn faintly green when a word of warning as to their health is needed. This stone appeases hate between those who once were friends and brings together lovers who have quarrelled. December people should marry those born in June.